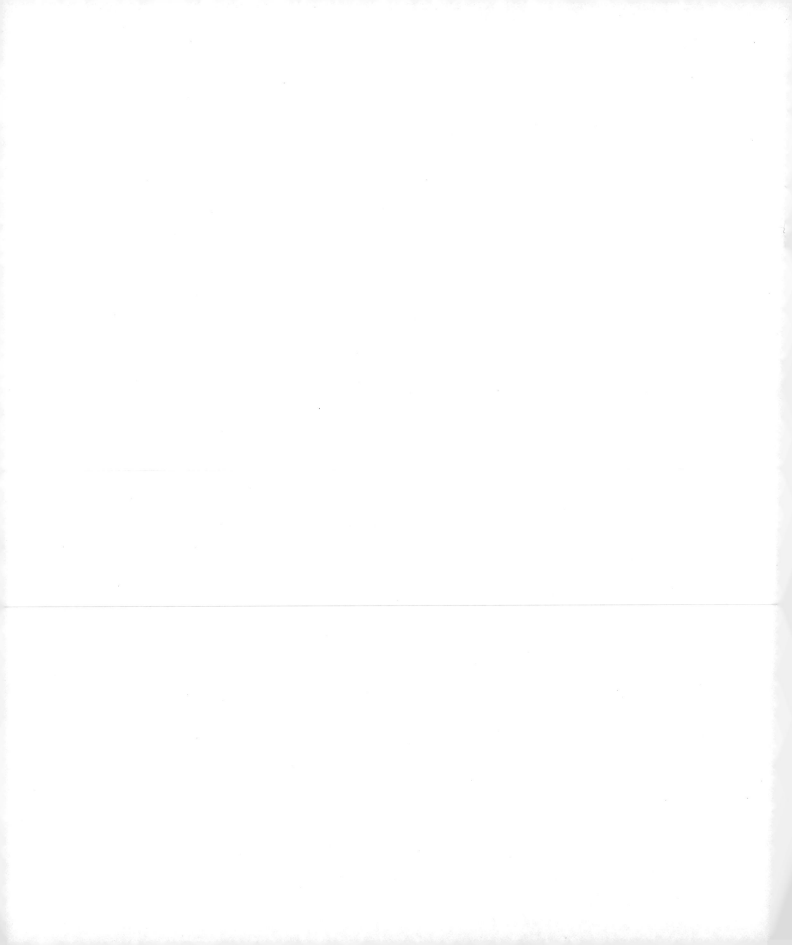

The First Rainbow

For our Mums,
with thanks for being there
S.B. & S.P.

The
First Rainbow

Su Box
Illustrations by Susie Poole

LION
Children's Books

Long ago, the people on earth were being bad. This made God very sad. He wanted to wash his world clean again. He would make it rain.

But there was one good man. His name was Noah.

'Build a boat,' God said to Noah.
'A boat to float when it rains, for
water will flood the earth.'
So Noah did.

'Fill the boat with animals.
Two of every kind,' God said
to Noah.
So Noah did.

There were all kinds
of birds and animals:

BIG and small...

FIERCE and friendly...

FURRY and smooth...

NOISY and *quiet.*

At last all the animals were on board.
There was just enough room for Noah
and his family too.
Then God shut the door of the boat.

It began to rain.
It rained for forty days.
It rained for forty nights.

Down, down, down fell
the rain.
Up, up, up rose the water.

Soon the boat was afloat.
Noah could see nothing
but water everywhere.

At last it stopped raining.

Days passed.

Weeks passed.

Months passed.

But still there was water everywhere.

The birds and animals were bored.

They tru**mpeted**...

and **grunted**...

and b l e a t e d...

and *BRAYED*.

One day the boat stopped on a mountain top. The water was going down!

Noah let a raven fly from the boat. It did not come back.

Then Noah let a dove fly from the boat. It came back with a leaf in its beak. Plants were growing. The land was dry!

The birds and animals
wanted to go outside.

They **chattered**...

and c h e e p e d...

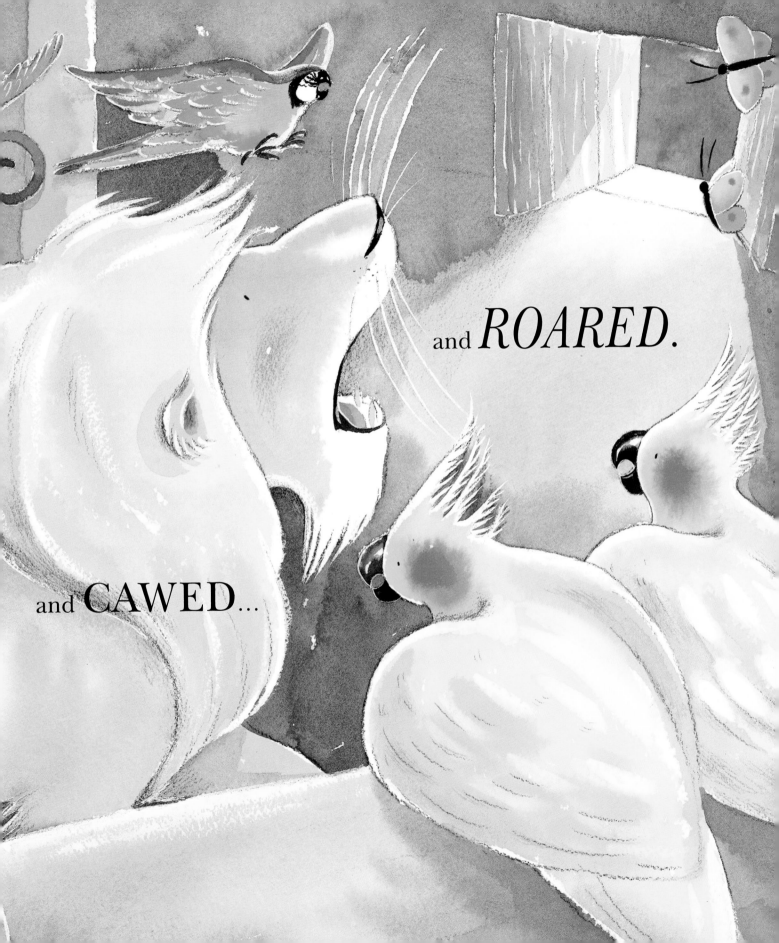

and ROARED.

and CAWED...

'Come out!' God said to Noah. 'The world
is clean again. Now you and your family and
all the animals must fill it with new life.'

'Thank you, God,' said Noah,
'for keeping us safe.'

So the birds and
animals left the boat:

creeping
and *crawling*...

running and jumping...

soaring

and diving...

slithering
and *shuffling*.

Then God painted
the world's first rainbow as
a promise that he would never
send a flood like that again.
He was happy with his clean,
new world.

Text by Su Box
Illustrations copyright © 2000 Susie Poole
This edition copyright © 2001 Lion Publishing

The moral rights of the author and illustrator
have been asserted

Published by
Lion Publishing
4050 Lee Vance View, Colorado Springs,
CO 80918, USA
ISBN 0 7459 4100 1

First UK edition 2000
First US edition 2001
1 3 5 7 9 10 8 6 4 2 0

Library of Congress CIP data applied for

Typeset in 18/28 Baskerville BT
Printed and bound in Malaysia